When God Says "No"

When God Says "No"

*

Understanding the Fatherhood of God

Roderick L. Evans

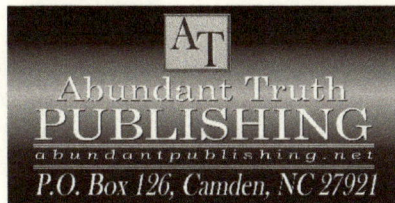

AT

Abundant Truth
PUBLISHING
abundantpublishing.net

P.O. Box 126, Camden, NC 27921

When God Says "No"
Understanding the Fatherhood of God

Front & Back Cover Designs by Abundant Truth Publishing

Abundant Truth Publishing
an imprint of Abundant Truth International Ministries

For information address:
Abundant Truth International
P.O. Box 126
Camden, NC 27921

ISBN: 978-1-60141-304-8

Contents

Contents (Cont.)

Contents (Cont.)

Preface

Believers experience disappointment and frustration while seeking God's direction and provision for their lives. Sometimes, it is because God's response is unfavorable. The information presented in this book comes from my personal experiences with the Lord.

There have been times when I did not receive the answer that I had expected. However, a revelation of His wisdom, grace, and love helped me to understand that He was not only my God, but my Father. This understanding helped me to stand in faith even when God said "No."

Roderick L. Evans

Introduction

Have you ever wanted something so much that you could almost taste or touch it? Have you ever wanted something so badly that the wait seemed like an eternity? Have you ever hoped for something greatly, only to discover that you would not receive the object of your hope?

The Bible is full of promises given to man by God. One of those promises is that God will give us what we ask for in prayer. However, there are times when we petition God that we do not receive the request. Some may feel hurt, disappointed, angry, and disillusioned with God. Others may feel confused, wondering, "Why God didn't give me what I asked for?"

We can understand a negative response from the Lord if we are asking for carnal, selfish, and unnecessary earthly things. However, there are times when God's response is "No," when we ask for healing and deliverance from extremely difficult situations.

In the pages of this book, we want to explore reasons why God's answer to us is not always right in our eyes. We will examine causes for the Lord denying the request of our hearts. In addition, we will learn how God's seemingly unfavorable response to us in certain requests is actually a demonstration of His love, care, and concern for us. This will lead us to a greater understanding of the Fatherhood of God in the life of the believer.

Chapter 1

◆

My Grace is Sufficient for Thee

- 2 Corinthians 12:9

Anyone who competes in athletics understands the importance of endurance. Endurance keeps the individual motivated even when the road to victory is rocky. Numerous athletes, through endurance, overcame the obstacles and went on to success in the competition. Christians can learn from the athlete's example.

The believer faces many trials, tests, and temptations. The scriptures attest to the fact that the righteous will experience afflictions.

Many are the afflictions of the righteous: but the Lord delivereth him out of them all. (Psalms 34:19)

Though the believer is consistently assured of God's provision and protection, he is not exempt from the troubles that life can bring. Therefore, the believer needs the strength and power to endure all that life brings. If the believer tries to endure and overcome on his own, he will fail. He needs the strength that can only come from God.

Through the Holy Spirit, man receives access to the power of God. Because of this, Paul could encourage the believers to be strong in the Lord.

Finally, my brethren, be strong in the Lord, and in the power of his might. (Ephesians 6:10)

However to walk in the strength of the Lord, the believer needs assistance. Therefore, God offers, His grace. Grace is a foundational part of the New Covenant. Yet, many believers do not understand grace. Therefore, a definition of grace is needed.

What is Grace?

We are saved by grace. We are recipients of God's grace. God gives us grace to do His will. Yet, what is grace? Any standard dictionary gives three basic definitions for grace.

1. A state of sanctification or regeneration enjoyed through divine favor.

2. A virtue coming from God.

3. Unmerited divine assistance given humans.

Based upon the revelation of the scriptures, we understand that the above definitions describe different aspects of the grace of God. In addition, we discover that grace can only come from God. It is not something we can develop or earn. It is supplied by God alone.

The first description of grace explains the work of grace in the salvation of man. Paul explained it in this manner,

> *For by grace are ye saved through faith; and that not of yourselves: it is the gift of God: Not of works, lest any man should boast. (Ephesians 2:8-9)*

Man receives salvation through grace. Though he may believe on Christ, God supplies His favor to make man's faith acceptable in His sight.

The second description of grace provides understanding as to how God uses man in His service.

> *Having then gifts differing according to the grace that is given to us. (Romans 12:6)*

He makes us vessels of His presence, power, and peace. It is through virtues imparted to believers as a product of His grace.

It is within the third description/definition of grace that the believer finds strength to endure difficulties. Grace is God's divine assistance and enablement given to men. *The foundation for handling God's "No" is rooted in the grace of God.*

Without God's grace, we will not be able to stand in faith and trust Him when He gives a seemingly negative response to our requests.

Paul and God's Grace

After defending his ministry in 2 Corinthians 10 and 11, Paul begins to close his argument in chapter 12. Following his description of previous revelatory experiences, Paul reveals that a thorn in the flesh was given to him to keep him humble.

> *And lest I should be exalted above measure through the abundance of the revelations, there was given to me a thorn in the flesh, the messenger of Satan to buffet me, lest I should be exalted above measure. (2 Corinthians 12:7)*

Paul revealed his thorn in the flesh to his readers as a balance to the defense that he had made for his ministry. Another reason for Paul's disclosure of the thorn in his flesh was that he wanted to explain why his bodily presence was weak. One of the prevailing arguments of Paul's opponents was that he wrote big and heavy letters, but when he would be present among the people, he was frail, weak, and did not speak very well.

> *For though I should boast somewhat more of our authority, which the Lord hath given us for edification, and not for your destruction, I should not be ashamed: That I may not seem as if I would terrify you by letters. For his letters, say they, are weighty and powerful; but his bodily presence is weak, and his speech contemptible. (2 Corinthians 10:8-10)*

It is our belief that Paul was defending his appearance and presentation. He wanted them to know that if he seemed weak and unassuming, it was for Christ's sake. Paul's thorn was present because it was the will of the Lord.

The Lord chose to allow one of the fallen angels (the messenger of Satan) to be the perpetrator of the thorn; that is, become the source of affliction in Paul's life. Paul's thorn was the result of permitted demonic activity against his physical body.

When Paul asked the Lord to remove the thorn, he did not receive the answer that he expected. God told him that His grace was all he needed.

> *For this thing I besought the Lord thrice, that it might depart from me. And he said unto me, My grace is sufficient for thee: for my strength is made perfect in weakness. Most gladly therefore will I rather glory in my infirmities, that the power of Christ may rest upon me. (2 Corinthians12:8-9)*

In essence, God said "No" to Paul's request. Paul asked that the thorn would be removed, but

God said He would give him grace instead. That is, He would give Paul divine assistance; though His response was not the one Paul was looking for. In order for Paul to endure God's "No," the grace of God was given. If we are to handle God's "No" and submit to the fatherhood of God in our lives, we need God's grace.

Accepting God's Grace

Handling God's "No" is something that every believer has to learn to do. We have established that as Paul needed God's grace, so do we. However, if we do not receive God's grace, it is useless to us. In order to accept God's grace, three things should be done: believe the scriptures, humble yourself, and receive by faith.

Believe the Scriptures

The Bible is God's revelation of Himself to

the world. It reveals the manifold dimensions of the character and nature of God. Within the pages of the Bible, there are references made to God's grace and its role in the life of the believer. However, without a belief in the scriptures, there can be no acceptance of God's grace.

To demonstrate a total trust in the scriptures, there must be first a trust in the **source** of the scriptures. We have to believe that God orchestrated the writing of the scriptures. Because of this, the scriptures can be followed without question of authority and authenticity.

All scripture is given by inspiration of God, and is profitable for doctrine, for reproof, for correction, for instruction in righteousness. (2 Timothy 3:16)

The Bible is a sure guide to eternal life. It provides us with the necessary tools for life and godliness through Christ. The scriptures are able to make us wise concerning our salvation. The key element to our salvation is the grace of God.

> *And that from a child thou hast known the holy scriptures, which are able to make thee wise unto salvation through faith which is in Christ Jesus. (2 Timothy 3:15)*

In addition to having a trust in the source of the scriptures, we have to trust the **authors** of the scripture. Some believe that God inspired the writing of the scriptures, but He used men. Therefore, their own opinions could have been interjected in the writings. However, this is simply not true. Consider the following:

> *Knowing this first, that no prophecy of the scripture is of any private interpretation. For the prophecy came not in old time by the will of man: but holy men of God spake*

***as they were moved by the Holy Ghost.
(2 Peter 1:20-21)***

Peter encouraged the believers by stating that the prophets (and apostles in his day) did not create the scriptures by their own will. They were moved by the Holy Ghost to declare (and write) God's counsel to man.

As believers, we have to believe that the authors of the scriptures were divinely inspired and could only record that which represented God accurately. Without this belief in the scriptures, we will not be able to accept His grace. Why? We will not trust God's testimony concerning grace as revealed in the scriptures.

There are individuals who can affirm their total trust in the scriptures. Yet, they fail to humble themselves and make practical application of the scriptures to their lives.

Humble Yourself

God offers His grace freely. Yet, some will not accept His grace to endure His "No" through stubbornness. It is similar to an individual who operates in unforgiveness.

We know by the scriptures that God commands the Christian to forgive. God does not tell us to do something that we are unable to do. His commands come with His strength and support to perform them.

However, some individuals will not forgive because they feel that if they do forgive, the offender is getting off without any consequence. The same applies to accepting God's grace when He says "No."

Some will feel that to walk in His grace and accept His "No" is to let God "off the hook." They feel disappointed and hurt and do not want to let it go. It does not matter even if it is God. Therefore, humility is needed to receive God's strength when He says "No." For, there will be times when He will give a negative response without explanation.

> **But he giveth more grace. Wherefore he saith, God resisteth the proud, but giveth grace unto the humble. (James 4:6)**

Thus, we will need to humble ourselves and receive His grace to handle His response to us.

Receive by Faith

The final key to accepting God's grace is to receive it by faith. Faith is vital to the acceptance of God's grace. Without faith, you will not feel that the grace of God is being supplied to you. Faith in God will make His grace tangible, even when you are experiencing disappointment from His response.

> *Now faith is the substance of things hoped for, the evidence of things not seen. (Hebrews 11:1)*

Faith makes God's grace attainable and discernable in difficult times; especially, when God refuses to give us a particular request. Faith causes the believer to go beyond what he feels into what God is actually doing. He does give grace to handle His responses.

Without God's grace, the believer will not be able to accept God's "No." As we go further into our discussion of the fatherhood of God, we must remember that all things can be received, believed, and achieved through His grace. We will now turn our attention to God, the Father.

Chapter 2

$$\blacklozenge$$

We Give Thanks to God and Father

- Colossians 1:3

There are depths and dimensions to the character of God. No one man has been able to comprehend and explain the manifold nature of God. Numerous attributes and accolades have been granted unto Him because of His greatness. However, one term cannot adequately convey who He is. While appearing to Moses, God did not give him a direct name for Himself. He said,

And Moses said unto God, Behold, when I come unto the children of Israel, and shall say unto

them, The God of your fathers hath sent me unto you; and they shall say to me, What is his name? what shall I say unto them? And God said unto Moses, I AM THAT I AM: and he said, Thus shalt thou say unto the children of Israel, I AM hath sent me unto you. (Exodus 3:13-14)

Moses asked God for His name. Yet, he receives a statement: *"I am that I am."* From this, we derive one of the names of God: Yahweh (or Jehovah). This name leads to three distinct attributes of His being.

Unchangeable Attributes of God

First, He is *self-existent*. This signifies that God exists because He exists. He needs no one to exist. Unlike the heathen gods in the surrounding countries, He did not need man's acknowledgement in order to exist. He reigns as God alone.

Remember the former things of old: for I am God, and there is none else; I am God, and there is none like me. (Isaiah 46:9)

God's self-existence demonstrates that He is *omnipotent* (all powerful). He exists based upon His own power and volition. God is perfect in power.

Second, He is **eternal** and unchangeable, and always the same, yesterday, to-day, and forever. Because He is self-existent, He has no beginning and end. He abides outside of time and the restraints of life and death. He is the creator of all these things.

For I am the Lord, I change not; therefore ye sons of Jacob are not consumed. (Malachi 3:6)

The unchangeable nature of God gives credence to the fact that God is *omnipresent* (everywhere).

Since He is eternal, everything about Him is eternal; including, His presence and personality. He will never change.

Third, He is **incomprehensible**. Moses would not have been able to describe the totality of God to Israel. Therefore, God simplified His response to Him. No one can understand the dimensions of His greatness or the depth of His understanding.

> **Hast thou not known? Hast thou not heard, that the everlasting God, the Lord, the Creator of the ends of the earth, fainteth not, neither is weary? there is no searching of his understanding. (Isaiah 40:28)**

The natural mind is unable to comprehend the fullness of God's greatness and power. This is because God is *omniscient* (all knowing). If He is the source of wisdom and knowledge, how can anything created by Him surpass Him in understanding? Any understanding that man has comes from what God gives.

Comprehension of the attributes of God should evoke fear, reverence, and awe in the hearts and minds of men. However, it does not always do this. Because God personally involves Himself in the lives of men, it is easy to lose perspective of who He is.

Though no name can adequately describe the fullness of the nature of God, there are two roles that He consistently demonstrates to men. He acts as God and Father.

> *A son honoureth his father, and a servant his master (Lord or God): if then I be a father, where is mine honour? and if I be a master, where is my fear? saith the Lord of hosts unto you... (Malachi 1:6, Parenthesis mine)*

God as a 'God'

We have affirmed that God's involvement with man is a personal one. *It is easy to lose perspective of who He is based upon His compassionate interaction.* Though the believer has intimate relationship with God, He is to be feared as God.

One of the prevailing concepts spreading today is that God is love, compassionate, and caring only. We can neglect His righteous and holy requirements. However, relationship with God does not exempt man from walking in righteousness.

Regardless of the religious persuasion, the gods that men created placed certain demands on their followers. The same is true for the God of heaven. If we serve Him according to His statutes, He will bless us. If we consistently rebel against what He sets up, we will experience His discipline.

Though the worship of God is practiced by men, it came not by the will of men. God instituted His own system of worship. In the wilderness, God revealed to Moses how He wanted Israel to come to Him as God.

God gave Moses the Law, with the Ten Commandments at its core. We can identify the three main areas of man's existence that the commandments addressed. The first was man's relationship with God. Israel was not to serve other gods.

Their worship was for Him alone. Unlike the surrounding countries, they were to serve one God. The majority of the countries worshiped more than one deity.

The second area addressed was man's worship of God. Israel was not to worship God in the same manner that the heathens worshipped their gods. They were not to create images or make vain oblation. In addition, they were not to offer their children up in sacrificial fires. The worship of God should remain pure.

The third area addressed was man's relationship with one another. They were instructed to treat one another with dignity and respect. They were to honor each other's families and property. God gave these commands while operating in the personality of God.

Under the New Covenant, the personality of God did not change, nor His statutes. *Some feel because the system of worship changed that somehow the righteousness of worship changed.* It did not. God still wants us to worship Him alone through Christ. Moreover, He still wants His worship to be pure, not mimicking the world. Finally, He still wants us to be righteousness in our thoughts and deeds.

If we do not honor and respect Him as God, we will live ungodly and unholy lives resulting in God's judgment in the Last Day. Therefore, we cannot neglect to respect, fear, and reverence Him as God. Some will disagree and say, "We are not to be afraid of God, but have an awe and reverence for Him." This is only partially true. God has to be loved and feared because He is a God. Consider the following:

> *And fear not them which kill the body, but are not able to kill the soul: but rather fear him which is able to destroy both soul and body in hell. (Matthew 10:28)*

> *He that despised Moses' law died without mercy under two or three witnesses: Of how much sorer punishment, suppose ye, shall he be thought worthy, who hath trodden under foot the Son of God, and hath counted the blood of the covenant, wherewith he was*

sanctified, an unholy thing, and hath done despite unto the Spirit of grace? For we know him that hath said, Vengeance belongeth unto me, I will recompense, saith the Lord. And again, The Lord shall judge his people. It is a fearful thing to fall into the hands of the living God. (Hebrews 10:28-31)

Though we are not to walk in fear, we should fear God for He does have the power to execute judgment.

The writer of Hebrews reminds the saints of how God punished those who disobeyed and despised the Law. He then asks, if they were punished in the covenant that passed away, how much greater punishment we will receive if we walk in disobedience in the New Covenant. Because He is intimate with us and demonstrates His compassion, do not forget that He is a God that requires righteous service.

God as a Father

In addition to His role as God, God is a Father. Not only did He create man, but also He relates to man as a father does to his children. Numerous scriptures attest to the fatherhood of God. We know that in the Book of Malachi, God refers to Himself as a father. Isaiah, prophetically, identifies God as a father.

> *A son honoureth his father, and a servant his master (Lord or God): if then I be a father, where is mine honour? and if I be a master, where is my fear? saith the Lord of hosts unto you... (Malachi 1:6, Italics mine)*

> *Doubtless, thou art our father, though Abraham be ignorant of us, and Israel acknowledge us not: thou, O Lord, art our father, our redeemer; thy name is from*

everlasting. (Isaiah 63:16)

However, there are differences in God acting as Father and acting as God.

As with any god, favor is gained based upon obedience and correct sacrifices. Therefore, the god's blessing is earned when the right rituals and ceremonies are performed. If God only operated in this manner, no one would be able to stand before Him. Even under the Old Covenant, God was merciful to Israel even after He gave them the consequences for sin. He did this because He was also a father.

In natural terms, a father disciplines a child in order to save him, not destroy him. ***The fatherhood of God brings balance to His role as God.*** In His role as Father, love is the primary motivation for His actions.

If He only related to us as a god, when we are wrong and disobedient, He would only punish and/or kill us. However, we know that when we are wrong, God disciplines us so that we will escape His judgment as God.

As a father, God's relationship with us is a personal one. It is not characterized by the impersonal relationship of a god and devotee/servant. God relates to us in an intimate manner though He is God. A father does not want to see his child go the wrong way or face injury. Therefore, God will endeavor to protect us, even if it is from ourselves.

As God, His righteous requirements are to be adhered to; but as Father, He disciplines rather than place final judgment upon us. Thus, when we understand God's role as a Father, we will understand how to handle his "No."

Chapter 3

The Firstborn Among Many Brethren

- Romans 8:29

God identifies Himself as God and Father. When He created man, it was in His image. Therefore, all men are His children, though all men do not relate to Him as Father. Because of this, God provided salvation to men through Jesus Christ. Though Christ and God are one, He related to God as a son would to his father. Christ came as a Son.

Numerous scriptures attest to Christ being the Son of God. Thus, it is within the person of Christ, the believer learns how he is to relate to God. Paul, in his letter to the Romans, presents a great mystery to the Church.

> *For whom he did foreknow, he also did predestinate to be conformed to the image of his Son, that he might be the firstborn among many brethren. (Romans 8:29)*

Above sacrifice and service, God wants man to conform to the image of Christ. His life is to serve as the model or example to all who receive Him as Savior. God intended for Christ to be the firstborn among many brethren. He serves as our Savior and Brother. The scriptures confirm this truth.

> *For both he that sanctifieth and they who are sanctified are all of one: for which cause he is not ashamed to call them brethren, Saying, I will declare thy name unto my brethren, in the midst of the church will I sing praise unto thee. (Hebrews 2:11-12)*

The writer of Hebrews informs us that those who are sanctified (the believers) and the one who sanctifies (Christ) are one. Thus, Christ is not ashamed to call us brothers. If we are brothers, then we share in relating to the Father as sons (this includes women).

In this chapter, we want to explore the sonship of Christ. In understanding Christ's relationship to the Father, we clarify our standing before Him. This will enable us to respond properly to His, "NO."

God & Christ's Sonship

Jesus Christ came to fulfill the will of the Father. God sent Christ, in the form of a son, to be an example. Jesus is God's Son and will be forever. God, Himself, testifies of the sonship of Christ.

He shall be great, and shall be called the

Son of the Highest: and the Lord God shall give unto him the throne of his father David. (Luke 1:32)

Before Jesus' birth, God revealed to Mary through Gabriel that Christ would be called the Son of the Highest. Regardless of the titles given to Jesus, none surpasses that of 'Son.' The Book of Psalms attests to this truth,

I will declare the decree: the Lord hath said unto me, Thou art my son; this day have I begotten thee. (Psalm 2:7)

In his defense at Antioch, Paul uses this verse to further substantiate the sonship of Christ.

God hath fulfilled the same unto us their children, in that he hath raised up Jesus again; as it is also written in the second psalm, Thou art my Son, this day have I begotten thee. (Acts 13:33)

After Christ's birth, God continued to declare that he was His Son. **At Jesus' baptism**, God spoke audibly in affirmation of Christ as His Son.

The gospels record this event. Matthew states,

> *And Jesus, when he was baptized, went up straightway out of the water: and, lo, the heavens were opened unto him, and he saw the Spirit of God descending like a dove, and lighting upon him: And lo a voice from heaven, saying, This is my beloved Son, in whom I am well pleased. (Matthew 3:16-17)*

Luke bears witness to this account,

> *Now when all the people were baptized, it came to pass, that Jesus also being baptized,*

and praying, the heaven was opened, And the Holy Ghost descended in a bodily shape like a dove upon him, and a voice came from heaven, which said, Thou art my beloved Son; in thee I am well pleased. (Luke 3:21-22)

And straightway coming up out of the water, he saw the heavens opened, and the Spirit like a dove descending upon him: And there came a voice from heaven, saying, Thou art my beloved Son, in whom I am well pleased. (Mark 1:10-11)

God testifies of Jesus that the world would know that He sent Him. Because of God's testimony, there is to be no confusion concerning Christ's relationship with the Father. When we change Christ's position with the Father or add our own thoughts, we say that God is a liar. John, in his first epistle, declares this fact:

If we receive the witness of men, the witness of God is greater: for this is the witness of God which he hath testified of his Son. He that believeth on the Son of God hath the witness in himself: he that believeth not God hath made him a liar; because he believeth not the record that God gave of his Son. (I John 5:9-10)

At Jesus' transfiguration, God testified again of Christ's sonship. After Jesus' clothes and face were changed, God spoke from heaven.

And was transfigured before them: and his face did shine as the sun, and his raiment was white as the light. (Matthew 17:2)

While he yet spake, behold, a bright cloud overshadowed them: and behold a voice out of the cloud, which said, This is my beloved

Son, in whom I am well pleased; hear ye him. (Matthew 17: 5)

Again, the Father speaks of His love for Christ while affirming His sonship. Not only does God the Father declare Christ's sonship, but also Jesus affirms His own sonship in relation to the Father.

Jesus & His Sonship

Since Christ is the firstborn among many brethren, He understood His role as Son. During His earthly ministry, He continually confessed that He was the Son of God.

At the age of 12, Jesus was separated from his parents. He was left behind at the temple reasoning with learned men concerning spiritual matters. When He was found, His response revealed His understanding of His relationship to God, the Father.

And he said unto them, How is it that ye sought me? Wist ye not that I must be about my Father's business? And they understood not the saying which he spake unto them. (Luke 2:49-50)

Jesus told Mary and Joseph that He must be about His Father's business. He knew that He came into the world to fulfill the will of Him that sent Him.

For I came down from heaven, not to do mine own will, but the will of him that sent me. (John 6:38)

After entering public ministry, Jesus would continually declare that He was the Son of God.

At the **scourging in the Temple**, Jesus referred to God as His Father.

And said unto them that sold doves, Take these things hence; make not my Father's house an house of merchandise. (John 2:16)

While reasoning with the Pharisees in ministering, Jesus defends His ministry by declaring that He (as the Son) could only do what He saw the Father do.

Then answered Jesus and said unto them, Verily, verily, I say unto you, The Son can do nothing of himself, but what he seeth the Father do: for what things soever he doeth, these also doeth the Son likewise. (John 5:19)

Jesus repeatedly affirmed His sonship and that God was His Father. He ministered to men as the Son of God. His relationship with God serves an example of the believer's relationship with God. Regardless of the ministry one has, it has to be done in subjection to the Father. If we miss this point, we will not understand the working of God in our lives. Consider the following,

> *Jesus answered, I have not a devil; but I honour my Father, and ye do dishonour me. (John 8:49)*

> *Say ye of him, whom the Father hath sanctified, and sent into the world, Thou blasphemest; because I said, I am the Son of God? (John 10:36)*

> *For I have not spoken of myself; but the Father which sent me, he gave me a commandment, what I should say, and what I should speak. (John 12:49)*

From the above references that Jesus made to the Father, we discover some important truths for the believers. The same manner that Jesus related to the Father as Son serves as the believer's standard for interaction with God the Father.

As with any father, there is discipline and instruction. These two things may not always be favorable from the child's perspective. However, the father knows what is best for that child.

Christ and God's "No"

Though Christ was Lord of all and He pleased the Father, there was a time when God did not give Him the response He wanted. The gospels reveal the turmoil of Jesus on the night He was to be taken into custody.

> *And being in an agony he prayed more earnestly: and his sweat was as it were great drops of blood falling down to the ground. (Luke 22:44)*

While awaiting His arrest and impending crucifixion, Jesus experienced sorrow and heaviness. He knew that He came to die, but now His suffering was at hand. Because of this, Jesus made a request to the Father. Luke records it on this wise,

Saying, Father, if thou be willing, remove this cup from me: nevertheless not my will, but thine, be done. (Luke 22:42)

Mark's account choosing different phrasing, but Jesus' request is the same.

And he went forward a little, and fell on the ground, and prayed that, if it were possible, the hour might pass from him. And he said, Abba, Father, all things are possible unto thee; take away this cup from me: nevertheless not what I will, but what thou wilt. (Mark 14:35-36)

Though Jesus came to die, He asked the Father to remove the cup (of suffering) and to deliver Him from that *hour.* In His request, Jesus stated that if God was willing, the cup could pass from Him. He plainly asked that it would be removed. Though He resigned Himself to do the will of God, His request was evident.

In His request, Jesus said that all things were possible unto the Father. Therefore, God could have allowed Jesus to escape the cross, and still offer salvation to man. How? The scriptures declare that with God all things are possible.

> *But Jesus beheld them, and said unto them, With men this is impossible; but with God all things are possible. (Matthew 19:26)*

> *For with God nothing shall be impossible. (Luke 1:37)*

And he said, The things which are impossible with men are possible with God. (Luke 18:27)

However, God rejected Christ's request. He allowed Christ to go to the cross for it would result in the salvation of man. **This helps us to understand one of the primary reasons that God will say "No" to our requests; that is, to fulfill purpose.** If the Savior had to accept God's "No," then the believer will also. Before exploring in detail reasons why God says NO, in the next chapter, we want to discuss the Christian's assurance in prayer.

Chapter 4

◆

Everyone that Asks Receives

- Matthew 7:8

What a wonderful promise given to the believer by Jesus! While delivering the famed, "Sermon on the Mount," Jesus reveals this assurance to the believer. We can pray in confidence, expecting to receive what we ask for.

> *Ask, and it shall be given you; seek, and ye shall find; knock, and it shall be opened unto you: For every one that asketh receiveth; and he that seeketh findeth; and*

to him that knocketh it shall be opened.
(Matthew 7:7-8)

God is willing to give us our requests, though there are times when He has to deny them. Though this book is designed to help when His response is No, this chapter is to serve as a reminder of the hope we should have in prayer. If we pray in a consistent manner, we can stand in expectation of receiving our requests.

Confess your faults one to another, and pray one for another, that ye may be healed. The effectual fervent prayer of a righteous man availeth much. (James 5:16)

The believer relates to God in various ways. Regardless of the manner, God offers us an assurance in prayer. However, in order to guarantee the reception of our requests, faith has to be in operation. In addition, our requests should align with the will of God for our lives.

Before examining the manners in which we relate to God in prayer, we want to briefly examine the role of faith.   Faith gives us access to our requests.

As long as we ask in faith, the Lord promises to hear us. Asking in faith demonstrates our trust in the Lord and His character. When we relate to Him, it has to be in faith.

Now faith is the substance of things hoped for, the evidence of things not seen. (Hebrews 11:1)

Faith confirms that we will receive our request. Faith serves as the title-deed for the things we are hoping for. Faith becomes the proof that we have received our requests, before they are ever manifested.

Then touched he their eyes, saying, According to your faith be it unto you. (Matthew 9:29)

The blind received their request for healing in proportion to their faith. Their faith was solid in the Lord.

And all things, whatsoever ye shall ask in prayer, believing, ye shall receive. (Matthew 21:22)

Jesus encouraged the disciples to believe (have faith) and they would receive whatever they asked. The same applies today. We must ask in faith. In this manner, the scripture will be fulfilled, "for everyone that asks (in faith), shall receive.

It has been stated earlier that believers relate to God in various ways. Each of these denotes a particular facet of the believer's relationship to God through Christ. When praying, we come to God in one or more of these ways.

The three most prevalent are as **servants, friends, and sons**. In each of these capacities, God gives us a promise that we will receive what we ask for.

I.   We are Christ's Servants

When we receive Christ, we become the sons (and daughters) of God. The Spirit of Christ baptizes us into the Body of Christ.

> *For by one Spirit are we all baptized into one body, whether we be Jews or Gentiles, whether we be bond or free; and have been all made to drink into one Spirit. (I Corinthians 12:13)*

However, our position as children of God, does not nullify the fact that we are to be servants of the

Lord. As servants, we can expect certain provisions from our master. Thus, there are times when we have fulfilled the will of God that we find ourselves in difficult situations.

> *For ye have need of patience, that, after ye have done the will of God, ye might receive the promise. (Hebrews 10:36)*

Yet, we can approach God, reminding Him of our faithfulness as servants, and expect Him to grant us our requests.

> *His lord said unto him, Well done, thou good and faithful servant: thou hast been faithful over a few things, I will make thee ruler over many things: enter thou into the joy of thy lord. (Matthew 25:21)*

In the parable of the talents, the servants that were faithful were rewarded. If we are faithful to the Lord in obeying His will, we can ask with full assurance of a granted request.

In the military, the government provides the soldiers with what they need for active duty. It is because the soldier is no longer responsible for himself. As God's servants, He takes responsibility for our needs, through prayer.

> *Who goeth a warfare any time at his own charges? (I Corinthians 9:7)*

As His servants, He will give us what we need (spiritually, physically, and emotionally) to fulfill His will.

> *Ye have not chosen me, but I have chosen you, and ordained you, that ye should go and bring forth fruit, and that your fruit should remain: that whatsoever ye shall ask of the Father in my name, he may*

give it you. (John 15:16)

After reminding the disciples of God's purpose for them as His servants, He encourages them. He informs them that as they bear fruit as productive servants, whatever they asked for would be given. The Lord will do the same for us as His servants.

II.   We are Christ's Friends

Jesus called the disciples friends. As recipients of salvation, believers become friends of God. Abraham was called the friend of God; then, we as his spiritual heirs are friends of God.

> *And the scripture was fulfilled which saith, Abraham believed God, and it was imputed unto him for righteousness: and he was called the Friend of God. (James 2:23)*

Thus, there are times when we approach God in prayer as His friends. We can approach Him in an open manner. In a parable, Jesus spoke of a friend's persistent request to another friend.

> *And he said unto them, Which of you shall have a friend, and shall go unto him at midnight, and say unto him, Friend, lend me three loaves; For a friend of mine in his journey is come to me, and I have nothing to set before him? And he from within shall answer and say, Trouble me not: the door is now shut, and my children are with me in bed; I cannot rise and give thee. I say unto you, Though he will not rise and give him, because he is his friend, yet because of his importunity he will rise and give him as many as he needeth. (Luke 11:5-8)*

Jesus tells a story of a friend petitioning a friend

for refreshments for some unexpected guests. However, the friend did not give him the request based upon friendship, but his persistence. This parable presents us with useful information as we approach God as friends.

The friend would not have made the initial request except there was a relationship between him and the other man. *The parable shows us that even as friends of God, we may not receive a prompt response to our requests.* However, we discover in this parable that because of the man's persistence, he received. This teaches us that we have to be confident, first, in our friendship with the Lord (as the man was in his friendship; else he would have given up). This will help us to be persistent when there is no immediate response.

And he spake a parable unto them to this end, that men ought always to pray, and not to faint. (Luke 18:1)

It is our belief that the man in the parable gave in to his friend's persistence because they were friends. We can be assured that God will give us our requests because we are His friends.

III.   We are His Children

Above the other ways in which we relate to God, the most prominent is that of sons. As a natural son approaches his father, we can approach God. Jesus set an example of how God will relate to us as His children.

> *And I know that thou hearest me always: but because of the people which stand by I said it, that they may believe that thou hast sent me. (John 11:42)*

While at Lazarus' grave, Jesus makes a profound statement in His prayer. He said to God that He knows that He always hears Him. As His children, the Lord will always hear our requests. Jesus spoke of the Father's willingness to grant to His children their requests while teaching.

> *Or what man is there of you, whom if his son ask bread, will he give him a stone? Or if he ask a fish, will he give him a serpent? If ye then, being evil, know how to give good gifts unto your children, how much more shall your Father which is in heaven give good things to them that ask him? (Matthew 7:9-11)*

Jesus asks a series of rhetorical questions. They were designed to show that a natural father is not going to give his son the complete opposite of what he asks for. Thus, if an ungodly individual can grant the requests of his children, how much the more will the Father give unto His children who make requests to Him? As sons (and daughters) of God, we can trust that God will give us our requests because He is good.

Regardless of the manner chosen to approach God (as servants, friends, and sons), we can expect to receive what we ask for. He will grant us our requests not only because of relationship, but also for His glory. Consider the words of Jesus:

> *And whatsoever ye shall ask in my name, that will I do, that the Father may be glorified in the Son. (John 14:13)*

God is glorified, through Christ, when He grants us our requests. Therefore, if He did not give us what we asked for, He would receive no glory. We can ask in faith, expecting to receive so that God can glorify Himself.

If all our requests are refused, how then could God receive glory, honor, and praise? Yet, He grants us our requests so that we can glorify His wisdom, power, love, and might. We can ask in faith and expect to receive.

Chapter 5

$$\blacklozenge$$

You Ask and Receive Not

- James 4:3

The Bible is full of promises given to man by God. We have discussed that one of those promises is that God will give us what we ask for in prayer. However, there are times when we petition God that we do not receive the request. Some may feel hurt, disappointed, angry, and disillusioned with God. Others may feel confused, wondering, "Why didn't God give me what I asked for?"

There are numerous theories concerning God's rejection of a request. Before examining scriptural responses to the above question, we want to dispel the prevailing erroneous belief surrounding God's **No**.

Misconception of God's No

The prevailing erroneous belief is that **sin** causes the Lord to reject our prayers. *It is true that God will withhold things from us if we are continuously rebellious.* However, as believers, the power of sin is broken and we are righteous in His eyes. When we sin, we sin as a righteous people that have erred and not as sinners that do not know God. It has been established that we are His children. If we are His children, through Christ, we have an audience with Him. The scriptures are clear concerning the depths of God's compassion.

Consider the following,

That ye may be the children of your Father

which is in heaven: for he maketh his sun to rise on the evil and on the good, and sendeth rain on the just and on the unjust. (Matthew 5:45)

But love ye your enemies, and do good, and lend, hoping for nothing again; and your reward shall be great, and ye shall be the children of the Highest: for he is kind unto the unthankful and to the evil. (Luke 6:35)

The above verses demonstrate clearly that God will bless even a sinner. How much the more will He hear us as His children, even when we err? However, the strength for the argument of sin as a reason for **NO** rests upon that which is found in Galatians.

Be not deceived; God is not mocked: for whatsoever a man soweth, that shall

> *he also reap. For he that soweth to his flesh shall of the flesh reap corruption; but he that soweth to the Spirit shall of the Spirit reap life everlasting. (Galatians 6:7-8)*

Individuals interpret these verses to mean that if we sin, then bad things are going to happen to us. Therefore, if we sin or err, we can expect negative things from life and God. However, this is not what Paul is teaching.

At the beginning of this chapter in Galatians, Paul speaks of restoring a brother who is fallen. Therefore, he is not condemning those who sin. In addition, he qualifies his statement in verse 8. After stating that one will reap what he sows, he lets us know what he is referring to.

If we sow to the flesh (sin), we will reap corruption.

He did not say God will reject our requests or that life will be bad. He simply means that our fleshly desires will produce a harvest in our lives. It will affect our spiritual life and productivity. When a natural child behaves badly, the parents do not stop taking care of the child. They do not stop giving the child what he needs. The same is true of God. When we sin, He does not leave us by ourselves. We are under a New Covenant with better promises.

> ***But now hath he obtained a more excellent ministry, by how much also he is the mediator of a better covenant, which was established upon better promises. (Hebrews 8:6)***

Under the Old Covenant, Israel's livelihood and blessing was dependent upon their obedience. When they sinned, God stopped blessing them. However, we are under a better Covenant. We become righteous by faith. Therefore, even when we fail God, we can stand in a position to receive from Him in prayer.

Now that we have discussed briefly the role of sin and God's **No**, we want to explore the reasons why God says, "No." Though there are numerous reasons surrounding God's **No**, three are clearly outlined in the scriptures. These will help us to understand the Fatherhood of God and accept His **No**.

Passion

We have determined that sin may not always determine a negative response. However, if we ask only to satisfy our carnal and selfish passions (lusts or desires), God will reject our requests.

> *Ye lust, and have not: ye kill, and desire to have, and cannot obtain: ye fight and war, yet ye have not, because ye ask not. Ye ask, and receive not, because ye ask amiss, that*

ye may consume it upon your lusts. (James 4:2-3)

It is true that God will grant us the desires of our heart. Yet, some requests that we make are only to satisfy the flesh. God has promised us that He will supply our needs. It is sometimes difficult for us to distinguish between the two. This is where frustration can set in. We may petition God thinking it is a need when it may not be.

Be not ye therefore like unto them: for your Father knoweth what things ye have need of, before ye ask him. (Matthew 6:8)

Jesus said that your heavenly Father knows what you need before you ask. However, the implication of His saying is that God determines what we need. Sometimes we make requests for things because someone else has it. At other times, our requests are only to make our lives convenient.

"Therefore, God may say "No" to certain requests because they are to make our lives convenient, rather than being a necessity."

Proper Time

Another reason for God saying **No** is timing. You may have the right request, but the wrong timing. In this instance, God's **No** is only for the moment. Yet, it becomes difficult to accept this when the situations are dire.

When bills are due, appointments are set, and illnesses worsen, we feel that God should do something immediately.

Since God sits outside of time, He knows all things and the outcome. He knows how to deliver and answer in a timely manner.

But when the fulness of the time was come, God sent forth his Son, made of a woman, made under the law. (Galatians 4:4)

Since the fall of Adam and Eve, men and women were left under the control of sin. Though wickedness and idolatry abounded, God still did not send Christ. Yet, the scripture states that when the *fulness of the time was come,* He sent Christ. This means the earth and the people present were ready for Christ to come.

However, this time was determined of the Father. It is the same with us. God will give certain requests when the fulness of times (for our situations) come. Until then, we have to accept God's **No.**

Purpose

God is a God of purpose. If God says **No** to

us because of it, we must discover what purpose is and why is it important.

Purpose: *Something set up as an object or end to be attained. Something that is proposed. An Intent or will. In terms of the Lord, purpose is the predestined plan and will of God.*

As we consider some truths concerning purpose, we will understand why God says **No** to us at times.

Purpose comes with Permanence

When our requests will take us off the path of our purpose in God, He will deny our request. We must understand that God's purpose for our lives is more than the fulfilling of an assignment. It also involves the development of our character as His children. ***Purpose is something that is ordained of God. It has to come to pass.*** When purpose is involved, God will do what is necessary in our lives to perform it.

> *...he which hath begun a good work in you will perform it until the day of Jesus Christ. (Philippians 1:6)*

Therefore, if our request will affect His predestined plan for our lives and ministries, He will say **No**.

Purpose Demands Patience

Because of purpose, God is patient with us. Even when we are disobedient to Him, He knows what we will become in Him.

> *Who hath saved us, and called us with an holy calling, not according to our works, but according to his own purpose and grace... (2 Timothy 1:9)*

Purpose causes God to be patient with us. Moreover,

purpose demands patience from us. We have to be patient with the Lord as His plan for our lives unfolds.

> *That ye be not slothful, but followers of them who through faith and patience inherit the promises. (Hebrews 6:12)*

He will deny our requests because He knows if we receive certain things that His purpose for our lives will not be achieved.

Purpose comes with Promise

If we submit to God's purpose, which includes His **No**, we have the promise of success in Him.

> *And we know that all things work together for good to them that love God, to them who are the called according to his*

purpose. (Romans 8:28)

It is impossible for God to lie (Hebrews 6:18). If we pursue God's purpose for our lives, it comes with the promise of His presence, power, and peace. However, in order for us to fulfill purpose, God will say **No** to us. He does it so that He can bless us as we fulfill purpose. *One key to enduring God's No is to understand that God will remember and reward us if we stand.*

We stated earlier that Jesus had to endure God's **No,** when He wanted to be delivered from the crucifixion. Jesus endured it because of the promise of His Father.

Looking unto Jesus the author and finisher of our faith; who for the joy that was set before him endured the cross, despising the shame, and is set down at the right hand of the throne of God. (Hebrews 12:2)

Jesus knew His acceptance of God's **No** resulted in the fulfillment of purpose. This was His *joy* because men would be saved. We should remember His example.

Chapter 6

$$\blacklozenge$$

And Will Be A Father Unto You

- 2 Corinthians 6:18

It is established that our Lord is God and Father. He does what He wants to do, when He wants to. Because of His love and concern for us, He denies us certain requests. He does this because He is a Father. In order to accept and appreciate God's **No**, we have to understand His Fatherhood. In both covenants, God wanted man to respect Him as God and relate to Him as a Father.

If we are expected to relate to Him as a Father, then He will deal with us as sons and daughters. In this chapter, we will explore God's relationship to us as a Father. In addition, we will discover how His role as Father requires Him to say **No** to us as His children.

> *Like as a father pitieth his children, so the Lord pitieth them that fear him. (Psalm 103:13)*

As a natural father has compassion upon his children, so does the Lord to the Christian. Again, we understand that God relates to us as a natural father does. From this, we can explore the fatherhood of God and how to cope when God says, "No."

Fathers Instruct Children

A natural father gives sound advice and instruction to his children. The same is true of God. As a father, His "No" comes to instruct us in the right paths.

> *Train up a child in the way he should go:*
> *and when he is old, he will not depart from*
> *it. (Proverbs 22:6)*

God knows the way that we should take. As a father, He will train us up. When He says "No" to us, it should challenge us to seek Him for an explanation. When we do this, God can instruct us concerning our lives and His requirements.

> *Wherefore come out from among them, and*
> *be ye separate, saith the Lord, and touch not*
> *the unclean thing; and I will receive you.*
> *And will be a Father unto you, and ye shall*
> *be my sons and daughters, saith the Lord*
> *Almighty. (2 Corinthians 6:17-18)*

The leaders of the Corinthian church wrote to Paul with many concerns. They wanted to understand what things were acceptable to God. They wanted to know what things they could expect to do and what they could expect God's approval upon. In his response concerning idolatry and unfruitful fellowship with unbelievers, he quotes the scriptures.

From this response, we understand that God was saying **No** to their request to be able to have unfruitful communication and fellowship with the ungodly. It was only in understanding God's **No** that they were able to be instructed of Him. Through Paul's response, we understand that the fatherhood of God required that they be separate from unbelievers and unclean things.

Sometimes, we will not receive God's instruction to us until there is something at stake. Therefore, God may say **No** to a request in order to pull us to the side to impart knowledge of His ways, wisdom, and works. To achieve this, prayer and communion with the Lord are required to understand God's **No** during this situation.

Fathers Discipline Children

In order to be an effective father, discipline has to be administered when necessary. There are numerous ways that a father may discipline his children. God, as a father, will discipline us. Sometimes He disciplines by rejecting our requests.

We stated earlier that a father does not want to see his child go the wrong way. A father wants his child to represent him and his name well. The name of God is attached to us. Through Christ, we become sons and daughters bearing His name and the seal of the Holy Spirit. As a natural father requires obedience from his children, so does the Father. ***When we are rebellious and in error, God may withhold certain requests from us until we are in right relationship with Him.***

For the Lord God is a sun and shield: the Lord will give grace and glory: no good thing will he withhold from them that walk uprightly. (Psalm 84:12)

The scriptures declare that God will not withhold any good thing from those who walk upright before Him. However, there are times when we are asking for the proper (good) things, but we have not obeyed Him. We become candidates for God's **No**. When Israel disobeyed God, He troubled them. He would not hear their request for relief until they turned.

I will go and return to my place, till they acknowledge their offence, and seek my face: in their affliction they will seek me early. (Hosea 5:15)

God stated He would not move on their behalf until they acknowledge their sin and turn to Him. The same holds true for us. God will supply us with what we need, but "requests" may be denied in order to bring us back into proper relationship with Him.

We should also remember that God's discipline does not always come because of disobedience. Sometimes it comes to make us more fruitful in Him. *Therefore, He may deny some requests to push us farther in our resolve to serve Him by faith and not because of His ability to grant us our requests.*

Fathers Protect Children

A natural father provides physical and emotional protection for his children. He desires for them to escape physical and emotional damage in their development. God's concern for us is similar to this. For this cause, God says "No" to protect us. What does God have to protect us from? He protects us from self, the sleight of men, and the sentence of death.

Protection from Self

A child does not know, at times, the things that will harm him. For instance, a child may want to hold something that is extremely hot. But, if the child receives what he wants, it will harm him. Thus, a father will withhold an object from a child to protect him. The same holds true of God.

There are times when we cannot see the potential harm if God granted us certain requests. So, God has to say **No** sometimes for our personal protection.

We do not know always how we will act and react if God granted us certain requests. We may be offended when He says **No**, but we will be grateful when we escape negative repercussions.

The heart is deceitful above all things, and desperately wicked: who can know it? The Lord search the heart, I try the reins... (Jeremiah 17:9-10a)

Since He knows the heart, He protects us from potential self-deception.

How shall I pardon thee for this? Thy children have forsaken me, and sworn by them that are no gods: when I had fed them to the full, they then committed adultery, and assembled themselves by troops in the harlots' houses. (Jeremiah 5:7)

God spoke and said that after He blessed Israel (fed them to the full), they rebelled. *Though we love God and want to please Him, the reception of certain requests may make us vulnerable to ungodliness*. Therefore , He will say **No** to protect us from ourselves.

Protection from the Sleight of Men

A father is selective about the friends of his children. He does not want them to be negatively influenced by peers. Most parents do not want their children to be followers. They want them to have their own minds and make independent, rational decisions. A father understands that not every person will be good **for** his child or good **to** his child.

If God grants us certain requests, it may put us in vulnerable situations with people. There are many individuals in the Body of Christ who feel lonely. They ask God to send them husbands, wives, and friends.   However, there are times when He will reject these requests to protect us. Some are not emotionally stable to handle certain relationships. Others may allow individuals in their lives to pull them away from God. So, God sometimes allows individuals to have few friends to protect them.

God does not want individuals to abuse and misuse us. Sometimes He will not allow certain people (though we ask Him to allow them to be in our lives) to be an intricate part of our lives so we will not be manipulated or controlled by them.

> *For do I now persuade men, or God? or do I seek to please men? for if I yet pleased men, I should not be the servant of Christ. (Galatians 1:10)*

Some will say, "I am not asking God for certain people to be in my life. How can other requests make me vulnerable in this regard?" If God grants us certain promotions on our jobs, positions in the Church, etc., it will cause us to have to interact with different kinds of people.

If we are not mature enough to handle new interactions based upon our environment, God may deny requests for promotions, changes in living status, or church affiliation. New blessings sometimes will bring us into new relationships. If we cannot handle these, God's answer may be **No**.

Protection from the Sentence of Death

God will judge the world. His final sentence is of death to the transgressors and sinners. Therefore, God will say **No** to us now in order to say **Yes** to us in that day. God protects us from others and ourselves so we will not be vulnerable to the enemy's deception. For we know his aim is to get men and women to share in his fate. The enemy will use our own fleshly desires and the influence of men to destroy our right standing with God. He knows that if we displease the Lord, God will judge us.

As stated earlier, certain requests are rejected if they will move us into ungodliness. This, in turn, will lead us to God's eternal   sentence of death if we do not repent. Some requests may never be granted. This happens because God is a Father who cares for His children.

We have to learn that God's **No** is not a sign of His anger, displeasure, or unfaithfulness, but an indication of His love. As a father loves his children, so God loves us. He said he would be a father to us. His fatherhood demands that He says "No." If we learn to appreciate His concern for us, we will not be offended and disappointed when God says **No**.

Chapter 7

◆

Hast Thou Considered My Servant Job?

- Job 1:8

The story of Job has been the subject of
controversy among biblical scholars for
years. There are varying explanations of its
authorship, focus, purpose, and spiritual
implications. The most popular use of his story
is to offer an explanation for why bad things happen
to good people. This is because Job is presented as
a righteous man who suffers greatly.

This book does not serve as an answer for why
we suffer. When considering this story, we must

remember that all the events that happened to Job were because of God's challenge.

> *Now there was a day when the sons of God came to present themselves before the Lord, and Satan came also among them. And the Lord said unto Satan, Whence comest thou? Then Satan answered the Lord, and said, From going to and fro in the earth, and from walking up and down in it. And the Lord said unto Satan, Hast thou considered my servant Job, that there is none like him in the earth, a perfect and an upright man, one that feareth God, and escheweth evil? (Job 1:6-8)*

When Satan responded to God, he made no mention of Job. However, God brought up Job's name. If God is perfect in wisdom and knowledge, He knew that Job would not curse Him.

He knew that the adversary's statements would prove to be false.

> *Then Satan answered the Lord, and said, Doth Job fear God for nought? Hast not thou made an hedge about him, and about his house, and about all that he hath on every side? thou hast blessed the work of his hands, and his substance is increased in the land. But put forth thine hand now, and touch all that he hath, and he will curse thee to thy face. And the Lord said unto Satan, Behold, all that he hath is in thy power; only upon himself put not forth thine hand. So Satan went forth from the presence of the Lord. (Job 1:9-11)*

Some others infer that God was proving something to the devil. We know that God is without equal and has nothing to prove. Then why did He allow such things to happen to Job? It was for Job's sake. Job's relationship with the Lord was enhanced because of this trial.

Through Job's testing, we discover three areas in Job's life that were exposed: His motivation for serving God, His view of God, and His perception of himself. When God says "No" to us, these three areas in our lives are exposed. As we consider his story, more insight is given into why God's says "No."

While Job was being tested, he made two requests to God repeatedly. His first request was that God would take his life. His second request was that God would tell him why he was suffering. God's response to these questions was "No."

> *Oh that one would hear me! behold, my desire is, that the Almighty would answer me, and that mine adversary had written a*

book. (Job 31:35)

God did not allow him to die or give him an answer for his troubles. Because of this, Job was forced to look inward. ***God says No, at times, to reveal character.*** His **No** revealed Job's character and will reveal ours.

Job's Motivation for Service

At the beginning of Job's story, Satan said that Job only served the Lord because of his possessions. God allowed Job's possessions and his children to be taken away from him. This was his response:

> ***Then Job arose, and rent his mantle, and shaved his head, and fell down upon the ground, and worshipped, And said, Naked came I out of my mother's womb, and naked shall I return thither: the Lord gave, and the***

*Lord hath taken away; blessed be the name
of the Lord. (Job 1:20-21)*

Job's response revealed that his service to God was
from the heart. Even without God responding to him
as his testing continued, Job's willingness to serve
the Lord did not alter. Had Job only served the Lord
because of what the Lord had given unto him,
this testing and God's silence would have revealed
it. There are times that God says **No** in order to
reveal to us our motivation for service. *If when God
says No, we withdraw our praise and service to
Him, this means we only serve Him for what we
can receive.* Jesus confronted this attitude in His
ministry.

*Jesus answered them and said, Verily,
verily, I say unto you, Ye seek me, not
because ye saw the miracles, but because ye
did eat of the loaves, and were filled. (John
6:26)*

The multitudes followed Him because they ate and were satisfied. We have to guard against this mentality in our relationship with the Lord.

God is gracious and generous, but we cannot serve Him because of His willingness and ability to grant us our requests. Our service to God must be from a pure heart.

God is not obligated to give us whatever we ask for because we serve Him.

Again, God will say **No** to us in order to reveal our motivation in serving Him. It is imperative that our motivation in service is from the heart.

Job's View of God

Job's testing revealed his view of his God. From the scriptures, we learn that Job did not charge God foolishly. He did not blame God for his troubles.

> ***In all this Job sinned not, nor charged God foolishly. (Job 1:22)***

Job did not turn against the Lord. He maintained his righteous view of the Lord. At the end of Job's testing, God praised Job for speaking of Him in a proper manner unlike his friends. His view of the Lord remained balanced.

> ***Therefore take unto you now seven bullocks and seven rams, and go to my servant Job, and offer up for yourselves a burnt offering; and my servant Job shall pray for you: for him will I accept: lest I deal with you after your folly, in that ye have not spoken of me the thing** which is right,* ***like my servant Job. (Job 42:8)***

Even though Job never changed His view of God,

he allowed his friends to push him towards self-righteousness. Because of God's refusal to give him an explanation, Job defended his life and righteousness. In doing so, he inadvertently challenged God's right to allow the sufferings to happen to him. God has to rebuke him for this with a question: *Wilt thou also disannul my judgment? wilt thou condemn me, that thou mayest be righteous? (Job 40:8)*

When God says "No" to us, our true feelings about Him are revealed. Do we become angry? Do we feel rejected? Do we accuse God? Do we develop feelings of mistrust or even hatred? If your answer to any of these is yes, then God's **No** came to reveal and heal.

Job's Perception of Himself

When God says **No** to us, it reveals our

motivation for service and our personal views about Him. In addition, it reveals our perception of ourselves. We mentioned earlier that Job's friends caused him to defend his righteousness. This reveals to us the reason for God's testing of him. He wanted to ensure Job's humility.

Though Job was blameless before the Lord, he felt he was too righteous for the Lord to punish him. This is why throughout the book he demanded an answer from the Lord. He wanted an answer not to understand what was happening, but to prove to his friends that he was not a sinner.

> *So these three men ceased to answer Job, because he was righteous in his own eyes. (Job 32:1)*

Therefore, when God appeared to him, he received a stern rebuke for this mentality. We discover that God said **No** to his request for understanding because it would satisfy his selfish request. However, God's refusal to answer him led to a revelation of Job's self-perception. He was righteous and he **knew** it. So, God allowed another level of humility to be imparted into him.

When God says **No** to us, a revelation of self-perception is disclosed. Job became righteous in his own eyes, demanding an explanation from the Lord.

If we do not receive what we ask for, do we demand an explanation from the Lord? Does God have to justify to us why He says **No.** This means we have become righteous in our own eyes. In order to spare us from this, God will refuse to give us certain things to reveal it. If Job was not exempt from falling into self-righteousness, then there is a chance we will.

From Job's example, we discover that God will not always give us what we ask for. We learned earlier that God's discipline is sometimes revealed in His **No**.

> *Furthermore we have had fathers of our flesh which corrected us, and we gave them reverence: shall we not much rather be in subjection unto the Father of spirits, and live? For they verily for a few days chastened us after their own pleasure; but he for our profit, that we might be partakers of his holiness. (Hebrews 12:9-10)*

Yes, He does it for our benefit. Job was blessed physically, but the greater blessing was in his character. He became a greater partaker of God's holiness and humility. God will bless us in the end as He did Job. We will receive the same reward if we continue to follow Him even when He says **No**.

Concluding Thoughts

◆

Submit Yourselves to God

- James 4:7

There are many factors that influence God's refusal of a prayer request. We have discovered that if we ask for selfish reasons or out of the proper timing, we will not receive from God.

In addition, we have learned that if there are weaknesses in our view of God and ourselves, He may say **No** to reveal them. However, there are times when God will say **No** and we receive no explanation by prophetic word or scripture. When this occurs, we have to submit ourselves unto the

Lord.

Humble yourselves in the sight of the Lord, and he shall lift you up. (James 4:10)

Trust His Character

It becomes an issue of trust. We have to trust in His character. This is the only way we can submit to God when He refuses to grant us certain requests. There are three things that govern the character of God: *holiness, righteousness, and love.*

But let him who glories glory in this, that he understands and knows Me (personally and practically, directly discerning and recognizing My character), that I am the Lord Who practices loving-kindness, judgment and righteousness in the earth;

for in these things I delight, says the Lord.
(Jeremiah 9:24)

When God says **No**, His *holiness* ensures us that He is not doing it in a malicious manner. His *righteousness* ensures that He will be glorified in the situation. Moreover, *His* love ensures that He is saying **No** with our best interest in mind.

Submit to His Will

We have discussed that Jesus submitted to God's will for His life. We have to follow His example. His response was, ***nevertheless not my will, but thine, be done. (Luke 22:42)***

Even if we do not understand or agree with God's **No,** let Christ's response become our own. In spite our personal feelings, Lord we want Your will to be done and not ours. The Lord's Prayer should become ours when God says "No."

After this manner therefore pray ye: Our Father which art in heaven, Hallowed be thy name. Thy kingdom come. Thy will be done in earth, as it is in heaven. Give us this day our daily bread. And forgive us our debts, as we forgive our debtors. And lead us not into temptation, but deliver us from evil: For thine is the kingdom, and the power, and the glory, for ever. Amen. (Matthew 6:9-13)

www.ingramcontent.com/pod-product-compliance
Lightning Source LLC
Chambersburg PA
CBHW030758150426
42813CB00068B/3226/J